HAL•LEONARD

INSTRUMENTAL PLAY-ALONG

AUDIO ACCESS INCLUDED

PLAYBACK+
Speed • Pitch • Balance • Loop

TROMBONE

MUSIC FROM ALL NINE FILMS

T0057801

Audio arrangements by Peter Deneff

To access audio, visit:
www.halleonard.com/mylibrary
Enter Code
4981-2444-2276-3976

ISBN 978-1-70510-715-7

HAL•LEONARD®

Visit Hal Leonard Online at
www.halleonard.com

Contact us:
Hal Leonard
7777 West Bluemound Road
Milwaukee, WI 53213
Email: info@halleonard.com

In Europe, contact:
Hal Leonard Europe Limited
42 Wigmore Street
Marylebone, London, W1U 2RN
Email: info@halleonardeurope.com

In Australia, contact:
Hal Leonard Australia Pty. Ltd.
4 Lentara Court
Cheltenham, Victoria, 3192 Australia
Email: info@halleonard.com.au

ACROSS THE STARS
(Love Theme from *"STAR WARS: ATTACK OF THE CLONES"*)

TROMBONE

Music by JOHN WILLIAMS

AHCH-TO ISLAND

from *STAR WARS: THE LAST JEDI*

TROMBONE

Music by JOHN WILLIAMS

BATTLE OF THE HEROES

from *STAR WARS: REVENGE OF THE SITH*

TROMBONE

By JOHN WILLIAMS

CANTINA BAND

from *STAR WARS: A NEW HOPE*

TROMBONE

Music by JOHN WILLIAMS

DUEL OF THE FATES
from *STAR WARS: THE PHANTOM MENACE*

TROMBONE

Music by JOHN WILLIAMS

THE FOREST BATTLE

from *STAR WARS: RETURN OF THE JEDI*

TROMBONE

Music by JOHN WILLIAMS

HAN SOLO AND THE PRINCESS

from *STAR WARS: THE EMPIRE STRIKES BACK*

TROMBONE

Music by JOHN WILLIAMS

THE IMPERIAL MARCH
(Darth Vader's Theme)
from *STAR WARS: THE EMPIRE STRIKES BACK*

TROMBONE

Music by JOHN WILLIAMS

MARCH OF THE RESISTANCE

from *STAR WARS: THE FORCE AWAKENS*

TROMBONE

Music by JOHN WILLIAMS

MAY THE FORCE BE WITH YOU

from *STAR WARS: A NEW HOPE*

TROMBONE

Music by JOHN WILLIAMS

THE RISE OF SKYWALKER

from *STAR WARS: THE RISE OF SKYWALKER*

TROMBONE

Composed by JOHN WILLIAMS

PRINCESS LEIA'S THEME

from *STAR WARS: A NEW HOPE*

TROMBONE

Music by JOHN WILLIAMS

REY'S THEME

from *STAR WARS: THE FORCE AWAKENS*

TROMBONE

Music by JOHN WILLIAMS

STAR WARS
(Main Theme)
from *STAR WARS: A NEW HOPE*

TROMBONE

Music by JOHN WILLIAMS

THRONE ROOM *and* END TITLE

from *STAR WARS: A NEW HOPE*

TROMBONE

Music by JOHN WILLIAMS

YODA'S THEME

from *STAR WARS: THE EMPIRE STRIKES BACK*

TROMBONE

Music by JOHN WILLIAMS